Association Chapter Systems: From Frustrating to Fruitful

By Cecilia Sepp, CAE, ACNP

"Unity is strength... when there is teamwork and collaboration, wonderful things can be achieved."
Mattie Stepanek, American poet, author, and speaker

ISBN: 978-1-944616-45-8
Copyright ©2024 by Cecilia Sepp
All rights reserved
Published by Broken Column Press
BrokenColumnPress.com

Praise for *Association Chapter Systems: From Frustrating to Fruitful*

"Unlock a fresh perspective with Cecilia Sepp's transformative guide. Dive into a reimagined vision of Chapter relations and discover the true value within. Embrace the insights, let them inspire you, and take action!"

       Michael A. Butera
       Founder and CEO - Association Activision. LLC

"Relationships are built on trust. Cecilia Sepp, CAE, ACNP, clarifies how to instill trust while evaluating how best to maximize chapters, affiliates, and components. A successful association understands the dynamics of chapters, components, or affiliates and maximizes them to increase member value. Sepp clarifies the right mindset and considerations for success."

       Cheryl Ronk, CAE, FASAE
       So Right, LLC

"This delightful read is like having a conversation with Cecilia and gaining instant access to her insight and experience as a chapter relations professional as she shares both strategic and very hands-on practical help. I especially like how she describes and defines the role, including, 'the goal is to build strong partnerships, provide a good volunteer experience, and strengthen the organization through positive action. Building bridges between the Chapters and the National Committees deepens the member experience and raises awareness of the value of local participation.' And I also heartily support this forward-looking observation, 'It is crucial to promote evolution in chapters and local networking options to survive in an increasingly noisy world that offers smaller and smaller niche groups for connection and self-identification.' This book is especially timely as many associations are now examining governance structures and, as Cecilia points out, the outdated chapter structure is ripe for a refresh."

       Barbara J. Armentrout, CAE

"If your role requires you to work with your organization's chapters, Cecilia Sepp's new book is a must-read.

"Cecilia says the things that many associations don't want to hear – that the chapter model is outdated, the relationship between national and chapters needs to change, and trying to force uniformity across chapters is no longer useful. These insights may be difficult to accept because they challenge the status quo, but for organizations that are open to new ideas, a path forward is revealed. That path is paved with collaboration instead of oversight, flexibility instead of rigidity, and innovation instead of maintenance.

"One of my favorite things about this book is that old-fashioned thinking is called out with such clarity, but more importantly, viable alternatives are offered. We're not left with only criticism. Instead, we gain a new way of thinking that encourages engagement and chapter growth."

> **Joy Duling, Founder/CEO**
> **journeycare.app**
> **joyofmembership.com**

"Cecilia explains the challenges and opportunities of association chapter relations; the ins and outs; the nuts and bolts; the right and wrong; the what works and what doesn't; and how to fix it. This book is an association road map – or should I say GPS – for successful chapter relations that ultimately benefit members."

> **Bruce Rosenthal**
> **Corporate Partnerships Strategist and Consultant**

Table of Contents

Introduction i
In The Beginning: How I Became a CRP 1
Why Do Associations Have Chapters? 9
An Overview of Chapter Relations 11
Chapter Relations Skills & Awareness Checklist 17
Chapter Role in Organization 19
Subordinate in the IRS Code and the Group Tax Exemption 23
Chapter Relationship Building and Management 29
Chapter Models: Bylaws and Boards and Bank Accounts 33
Chapters or Affiliates: Comanches or Mongols? 39
Chapter Guidelines 43
Rogue Chapters 47
Tracking Chapter Bank Accounts 51
Dissolving Inactive Chapters 55
Supporting Chapters with Current Technology 61
Chapter Leadership Training 65
Chapter Leadership Councils 69
Chapters and Strategic Planning: Work Together for Stronger Mission Impact . 73
Is your Chapter System Really That Bad? 83
Chapter Structures Continue to Frustrate Associations – So Let them Go 85
Re-Imagining Chapter Systems 87
A New Way Forward 89
About the Author 93

Cecilia Sepp, CAE, ACNP
Introduction

Chapters are near and dear to my heart. I spent over 15 years as a chapter relations professional and I loved it. I worked in different models with different requirements so I got to see the good, the bad, and the ugly. I also saw a lot of the unnecessary actions that we like to think are guiding and supporting chapter leaders but is activity for the sake of looking like you are doing something.

Much of what we "require" chapters to do today wastes their valuable volunteer time. Rather than filling out forms or writing reports, they should be creating valuable experiences locally. Chapter relations professionals should be supporting activity that supports a valuable member experience, not dinging chapters because their quarterly update is late. That is a waste of the Chapter Relations Professional's time. Instead, the Chapter Relations Professional's time should focus on relationship management, education of local leaders, and advocating on behalf of chapters to the broader association.

Sadly, the focus is on bureaucracy rather than outcomes. I still hear many association professionals who work with chapters complain that they won't do what they are told or that they can't control them. You don't win hearts and minds by beating people over the head, but you do create a negatively tense situation that leads to disruption and lackluster experiences.

This is why chapter systems are frustrating instead of fruitful. We become more focused on the system rather than the people the system is meant to serve. Associations are, after all, the relationship industry. And relationships require a certain emotional investment that goes beyond the bureaucracy and feeds the soul of the members.

It takes a different type of commitment to be a successful chapter advocate. You must manage multiple relationships,

Association Chapter Systems: From Frustrating to Fruitful misunderstandings about your role in the organization, and find that balance between requirements and valuable experiences.

Many people in our profession don't understand this element of the chapter network experience – the Chapter Relations Professional brings together the members across regions and acts as their connection to the association's world of ideas.

My motivation to write this book is to bring my experiences and perspectives to those professionals managing chapter networks, especially those who are new to this position. I learned a great deal over the years about service, relationship management, and the role of chapters. There are not many books on this topic, and while there are many webinars and templates available from multiple sources, what I see missing is the heart – that certain "je ne sais quoi" as the French say. "That certain something" that is hard to define and is the difference between success and failure.

Contrary to some opinions, chapters are not a drain; they are an asset. To be successful at chapter relations, we need to have a basic understanding of how they work and why we have them. This book includes practical aspects of management, useful tips on relationship management, and helpful explanations for things the chapter relations professional doesn't think about every day, in addition to challenging the conventional wisdom with different thinking and suggestions.

My goal is that this book will inspire you to look at things with a fresh perspective, to understand how most chapter networks run, to realize the importance of strong relationships, and to ultimately become a change agent in the profession.

Cecilia Sepp, CAE, ACNP
In The Beginning: How I Became a CRP

Before I drag you down memory lane, I should explain what CRP means. It's an acronym, of course, because our whole profession runs on this wicked shorthand. CRP stands for Component Relations Professional or Chapter Relations Professional. When I started my career in nonprofit management, we used the term chapter relations to identify the area of practice for professionals working with local or state chapters of the national organization.

Over time, we (professionals in the chapter relations community) came to realize that many of our colleagues worked with not just chapters, but special interest groups (SIGs), committees, or other components of the organization where members could volunteer and contribute.

While the term became more inclusive, the focus is the same: supporting and serving volunteers in a variety of roles within the association. Organizations are made up of many parts and this offers opportunities for expanding engagement and increasing the value of the member experience.

Of course, I didn't know any of that when I was thrust into my first CRP job. I was just a chubby kid from South St. Louis, Missouri, who came to DC to make my mark on the world.

My first job in Washington, DC was at the US Chamber of Commerce working as an Assistant in the Policy Group. I started in the Resources Policy area, and then was "promoted" to be the Assistant to the Director of the Labor and Human Resources Policy Department. It was a great opportunity to learn about policy, management, and operations. (This was a promotion because I was working with a Department Leader instead of a policy manager.)

I really loved that job, as I was allowed to do a lot of things using my own judgment, as opposed to asking permission all the time.

Association Chapter Systems: From Frustrating to Fruitful

But then, my boss decided to take a new position as the Chief Staff Executive of the American Corporate Counsel Association (ACCA), which is now known as the Association of Corporate Counsel. I was really upset that my boss didn't offer me a position at his new organization, but I made the best of things at the Chamber and ended up getting a new position and promotion. Finally, I was doing policy work! I also was a lobbyist but didn't enjoy that part at all. Being from Missouri, I say what I mean and mean what I say – not necessarily an attribute for a successful lobbying career.

A few months after he left, though, my former boss took me out to lunch and said he had a position open that he would like to offer me if I was interested. He knew he could rely on me and he was looking to add me to his new team working as the Media Relations liaison and the Board of Directors contact, supporting his work with the board. Since we had a good working relationship previously, and my career arc at the Chamber was stagnant, I accepted. However, I did learn you shouldn't follow a boss to another organization unless they ask you to come with them at the beginning. Coming in later creates all kinds of unnecessary drama related to other people's issues.

But taking that job was a watershed: That is when I walked through the door from policy work to the wacky world of association management.

This all happened a long time ago, so I'm not trying to accurately remember titles or dates; the point of the story is that I started at ACCA in one position that I enjoyed (media liaison and board support) but was suddenly assigned to a chapter relations position due to a staff member going on maternity leave.

Of course, I had no idea what I was doing when it came to chapter relations. I wasn't even sure what it was or what it meant. I was about to receive a crash course in working with local volunteers.

Since the staff member was planning to return to work after her baby was born, I accepted the position thinking it was temporary. **The problem with the new assignment was that I turned out to be good at it, so it became my permanent position.** Despite becoming good at chapter relations over time, there were some bumps in the road at the beginning.

My supervisor at the time was the Director of Communications and Marketing, but she also oversaw membership, which include the association's chapter network. I met with her to get advice on how to get started. At the time I began this role, ACCA had 30 to 40 chapters across the United States. Again, a long time ago, so I don't remember the specifics. **My supervisor advised me to get the list of all the chapter presidents, call them, introduce myself, and ask them what they needed**. A practical way to begin, and it gave me some direction.

I started dialing the phone. Yes, dear reader, at the time, we had actual phones with handsets and buttons you could actually push. **Very cool when you had to hang up on someone because slamming the handset down made a very satisfying sound**.

By the time I finished calling all the chapter presidents, I was pretty discouraged. Almost every single phone call went the same way: Why are you bothering me? Just send me my rebate check and leave me alone.

What the heck had been going on here? And was I the person that could fix this?

I reported these grim results back to my supervisor and sought her advice on what to do next. She said, "We will kill them with kindness," and that is what we set out to do.

Unbeknownst to us when I received this assignment, the previous chapter relations director did not do a good job managing the network and the relationships. Often when chapters asked for help, the response they received was, "No." They become frustrated, annoyed, and a little angry. **No wonder they just wanted to get their money and be left alone!**

Over time, I followed the direction of my supervisor and did everything I could to improve relationships with the local chapters. I talked to them. We created a printed Chapter newsletter to share information across the network. We improved the structure of our Chapter Presidents Council so that it made real contributions to the organization.

Chapter guidelines were in place, but we updated them and kept them top of mind for the local leaders. As things progressed, we added a weekly fax newsletter called "Chapter & Verse" that shared current news and highlighted the activities of individuals. It was a great way to support the microvolunteering program I had started too because I could highlight the varied member engagement opportunities we offered. At the time, I didn't realize I was running a microvolunteering program – it just made sense to offer different levels of volunteer commitment. It's why I often joke that if I realized I had invented microvolunteering, I could be rich by now.

We rebooted the chapter regions and held quarterly update calls with their national board liaisons; each region had a board member assigned to it. Rebuilding the relationships and reintegrating the chapter network into the organization led to increased local activity and an increase in the number of chapters. Assigning board members to act as regional liaisons also increased the value of board service as it provided more options for directors to get involved. It allowed board members to meet more local leaders, which helped identify potential future board members.

The regional calls were a humorous but wonderful validation of the improved relationships and amount of trust we built. Each quarter, the board liaison for a chapter region would convene a conference call and give updates to the Chapter Presidents. I would write talking points and share them with the liaison so they knew more details about what was happening.

On one call, **I realized to my horror that the board liaison was reading word for word the talking points I sent her!** I didn't say anything and let the call go on – until someone had a question about one of the talking points. The board liaison said, "I don't know – I'm just saying what Cecilia told me to say." Whoa. **Talk about not realizing the influence I had created within the Chapter network.**

I jumped in the conversation and pointed out these were talking points to help the liaison lead the call (not something to be repeated because I said so!) and answered the question. **It was an important lesson in understanding the power of trust.** If it is too strong, you can create a situation where people don't question. That's never a good thing. This is one of the most important lessons any staff member who works with volunteer networks should learn: **NEVER abuse your role or your power for personal gain**. I've seen organizations where this has happened and it leads to negative feelings, increased tensions, and a misdirection of energy. As staff, we are here to serve. We are not here to build private fiefdoms.

While it was startling, this situation did show me that the years of work had paid off and the network was thriving and strong because of the good relationships we built based on trust. That is the secret ingredient to successful Chapter programs – trust in each other, trust in the network, and trust that problems will be solved.

Within two and half years, I went from "just send me my rebate check" to being sought out by local leaders for advice and support. I was very flattered in one of these conversations to be referred to as the ""Great Demi-Goddess of Networks."" It was a hard-earned compliment demonstrating that with time, patience, and relationship management, we were able to work with our members to bring new energy into their work at the local level.

We (the volunteer leaders and I) became partners in improving the chapter governance system, increasing local activity, and building a pathway to national leadership.

By the time I left ACCA, we had 46 chapters and one of those was based in Europe. These were all active and established chapters because we had already dissolved the inactive chapters that couldn't be re-established. Creating a strong member network enhanced the value of membership and positioned the association for continued growth globally.

You might be wondering why I keep saying "I" in this story; that's because like a lot of CRPs, I was a department of one. While I worked with my fellow staff members on certain things, I was the one with the responsibility to serve our volunteers in our chapters.

> **CLARITY MOMENT**
>
> What works: Collaborating, Communicating, Connecting
>
> What DOESN'T: Dictating, Requiring, Demanding, Controlling

Eventually, I was given the responsibility of working with our Special Interest Groups too, which were called National Committees. It was a natural addition to my scope of work because working with volunteer leaders uses the same skill set and knowledge. You may apply it differently to a SIG than a chapter, but the goal is to build strong partnerships, provide a good volunteer experience, and strengthen the organization through positive action.

Building bridges between the Chapters and the National Committees deepened the member experience and raised awareness of the value of local participation. We created (working with the volunteers) the best task force I ever supported: The Chapter/National Committee Task Force on Synergy.

What synergy were we chasing? Local chapters needed content for events, and National Committees (remember, these were our version of SIGs) had content to share. We had a six-month window for this group to do their work. It was a collaborative and productive Task Force, and at their last meeting, since their mission was accomplished, they voted to dissolve the Task Force.

When was the last time you saw THAT happen in an association? Usually, the members vote to continue their work and task forces become committees. **But this group understood their mission and purpose and fulfilled it.** This led to stronger relationships across the organization and "Co-presentations" locally between Chapters and National Committees.

This is what happens when we tap into the true power of chapters: **collaborate, don't dictate**. They are the organization's partners, not their competition. It requires dedication and patience to create and maintain the relationships that are the member community but that is why they call our profession the relationship industry. Relationships are our most valuable asset in association management.

What we do in chapter relations is intangible, yet it is, in my opinion, one of the most valuable parts of any association. Ideas inspire people to action, not performance guidelines.

What I learned over the years from successfully working with chapters is this: Collaborate. Communicate. Connect. And sometimes a little cajoling helps too.

What doesn't work? Dictating. Requiring. Demanding. Controlling. That is the fastest way to create problems that don't need to exist.

Where do chapters fit in when it comes to association management? Let's explore the broader profession and how chapters can support mission fulfillment, governance structures, and content delivery.

Three Main Chapter Responsibilities

- Communicate National Organization Goals and Programs
- Represent your Chapter: make your concerns known
- Work to engage Chapter Members in the Organization

Cecilia Sepp, CAE, ACNP

Why Do Associations Have Chapters?

Building on the context of the nonprofit status, we need to understand the differences within the 501(c) status itself. Most people don't realize that there are 29 501(c) status definitions[1] in the IRS Code, which means there is something for everyone who wants to make the world a better place.

Clarity Moment: Too often, people (even in the nonprofit management profession) use nonprofit and association as if they are two different things. **THIS IS NOT ACCURATE**. All 501(c) organizations are nonprofit; *it is what TYPE of nonprofit you are* that defines your organization's structure, governance system, and advocacy program.

In practical terms, there are 3 nonprofit status types that are the most common and have some awareness within the public:

501(c)3: foundations and charities (most common and best known)

501(c)4: policy-driven organizations

501(c)6: professional societies or trade associations

The 501(c)3 would not have a chapter model because their structure does not use a membership model. Foundations and charities build relationships and communities with donors and supporters that support the mission, and there is not a need to "join." Unfortunately, you will see some "membership organizations" that are incorporated as a 501(c)3 – this is not the best designation, as it leads to confusion about what is and isn't tax deductible, and more importantly, a 501(c)3 has stricter guidelines on lobbying than other 501(c) groups. Lobbying is an important benefit of "membership" that cannot be delivered as well in the 501(c)3 model.

---

[1] https://www.irs.gov/charities-non-profits/other-tax-exempt-organizations

Some 501(c)4 organizations might want to use chapters because their goal is to promote policies on different areas of society such as tax policy, first amendment rights, or public transportation. Chapters could be useful in spreading the word locally, but these groups tend toward a donor/supporter model rather than a membership model, so a chapter model is not necessarily the best approach.

When it comes to what type of 501c organization would have chapters, that would be the 501(c)6 model of professional societies or trade associations. This type of nonprofit organization is based on a "membership model," meaning individuals or organizations join and pay dues to participate. Dues are not tax deductible as a charitable donation but are tax deductible as a business expense.

Clarity Moment: Dues are NEVER tax deductible as a charitable donation – even if your membership organization is a 501(c)3.

Creating a chapter system or network in a membership model can add value and increase the depth of the member experience by providing more activities and connections locally. This opportunity to experience membership on a regular basis locally can create stronger ties to the organization by extending identity with the association outside of national conferences and webinars.

When I was a Chapter Relations Director, I always kept in mind the saying, "Chapters are where the rubber meets the road." **Translation: Members move the organization, so make sure to harness their energy.**

Cecilia Sepp, CAE, ACNP
An Overview of Chapter Relations

Chapter Relations is the practice of working with local and state chapters of your organization to move the mission forward. In most instances, Chapters are structured in a very similar way to the national association to serve as a local "mini-me"[2] of the group (more on the mini-me concept later).

When looking at the current approach to Chapters, it has not changed much in decades despite the opportunity to integrate the available tools and technology in the way we live now in the 21st Century. Most associations have requirements for Chapters to form and be officially recognized, and then the Chapters have to follow a list of guidelines in order to maintain their official status. If chapters don't "do what they are told" and fulfill a laundry list of responsibilities, there are punitive steps in place to modify their behavior. So why do I want to be a local leader?

What ends up happening is the creation of a complicated system that becomes tedious to maintain on both ends of the relationship. The Chapter is constantly working (or struggling) to meet all their annual requirements while recruiting volunteers. Instead of providing an interesting experience that provides new opportunities, this system can lead to our volunteers performing unpaid part-time jobs. Considering this unpaid work is not recognized all the time, it's a prime area for creating resentment and anger.

If the volunteer experience isn't fun, what's the point?

It seems associations continue to rely on the "best practices" of controlling, demanding, and telling chapters what to do. Instead of focusing on providing meaningful experiences, the national association focuses on the requirements, as if this is some sort of

---

[2] "Mini-Me" is a character created by Mike Myers in his "Austin Powers" spy movie series. He was a smaller clone version of Austin's nemesis, Dr. Evil.

privilege to be buried in reports and nagged constantly about "not doing what you are told."

That being said, my goal here is to get Chapter Relations Professionals, the C-Suite, and volunteer leadership at the Board level to think differently about Chapters and what they really represent.

> **Chapter:** local or state component that exists because the larger association exists
>
> **Affiliate:** separate organization in same profession/industry but exists on its own

Chapters and Affiliates matter at every level of the organization. If you are one of those C-Suiters who think they are a drain or a pain, you are WRONG. If you are lucky enough to have chapters, you have a tangible network that represents the connection we all have through our professional membership organizations. This connection is the most important reason that people join in the first place.

Overlook the power of this connection at your own risk.

Chapters give this connection PHYSICAL FORM in a virtual world. It provides form to the intangible idea of the membership association, and because it provides form, it contributes to function. I love a good Bauhaus reference.[3]

This bears repeating to clarify what type of network we have:

- Chapter: local or state component that exists because the larger association exists
- Affiliate: separate organization in same profession/industry but exists on its own

---

[3] The Art Story: Bauhaus -- https://www.theartstory.org/movement/bauhaus/

Cecilia Sepp, CAE, ACNP
Are Components the same thing as Chapters?

YES. But other things are components too like Special Interest Groups (SIGs), committees, task forces or working groups. Even the board of directors is a component because it is a part of the overall organization but the Chief Staff Executive (CSE) is the liaison to and partner of the board.

All of our volunteers share two of the most precious resources in the world: Time and Knowledge. Two important questions we need to ask ourselves as Chapter Relations Professionals are:

- What actions and thoughts can we adopt to bring us a broader understanding of what volunteers are actually giving us?
- How can we support them and acknowledge this?

This will give us insight into the most compelling Chapter Relations question today: **Is it time to sunset the current approach to Chapters?**

When considering this question, we need to review the need for duplicate mini-me organizations that are no longer serving the original purpose. Do we need to have chapter boards of directors, chapter committees, chapter newsletters, chapter bank accounts, and chapter elections? Or would this time and energy be better served supporting loca volunteers leading member experiences without the handcuffs of chapter requirements?

Considering how much money is sitting in Chapter bank accounts, untouched and therefore pointless, I think it is the responsibility of the national association to completely revamp chapters – even if that means eliminating them in favor of a different and hopefully better system.

Putting Chapters into historical perspective, this concept as practiced today originated in the 19th Century, a time when travel took weeks, months, or sometimes years, and it might take the same amount of time for a letter to get to someone. Members of organizations of all types only met every few years (see previous comment about how long it took to get places) and even though these meetings or conferences might last for months, how was the ongoing connection and work going to continue?

This led to the need for ongoing work by local chapters outside of these infrequent meetings and large gaps in communication. Therefore, it made sense to set up a local version of a national or international organization because they were doing that work where they lived, and it had to be done consistently.

However, we no longer live in that world – and we haven't for a really long time. We live in a world of instant communication, with frequent and fast travel options. It only takes 14 hours to fly to Australia from North America – that's the other side of the world! In the 19th Century, there were no flights because we hadn't perfected flying machines yet. To get to Australia in the 19th century, you would have to take a train to a port city where you would catch a ship. Sailing to Australia in the 19th Century took two to four MONTHS – and that is if everything went smoothly.[4]

Communication also took a long time. There were few if any telephones in the 19th Century, and letters or telegrams could take weeks or months to get to their recipients. You would then have to wait weeks or months for a reply. In this environment, having a local chapter of an organization made sense so that the work could continue during those long gaps in messaging.

We live in a world where travel is fast and easy and communication is almost instantaneous, yet we use a Chapter system

---

[4] https://museumsvictoria.com.au/immigrationmuseum/resources/journeys-to-australia/

that developed in an era of groups working in isolation for long periods of time.

We continue to have a quandary of wanting to have better Chapters but not wanting to stop doing "what we've always done."

While Associations may have adopted digital tools for communicating, *the driver seems to be saving money on paper and postage rather than on meeting members where they are.* Associations are missing many opportunities through chapters to connect, educate, support, and inspire their members. Why? Because they are too busy looking for chapter reports that confirm a certain number of requirements have been met. Is this delivering member value? Or is it just busy work?

When allocating resources, is this a good way to spend money, time, and staff energy? If the staff are supporting and encouraging a valuable experience, that is worth the investment. If staff spends time chasing reports and scolding local volunteers, then it's a waste *of everything* and will distract your organization from mission fulfillment. Wasted resources are lost forever – just like a member who has a bad experience.

Cecilia Sepp, CAE, ACNP

Chapter Relations Skills & Awareness Checklist

Navigating Chapter Relationships – Necessary skills include:

- Patience
- Diplomacy & Tact
- Ability to negotiate
- Communication skills
- Strong listening skills
- *Ability to see what is really causing the problem when one arises*

Attributes of Happy Chapters:

- Engaged
- Communicates
- Shares Information and Suggestions
- Files requested information without much prompting
- Partners with Association and other Chapters
- Advocates for Association Mission

Attributes of Unhappy Chapters:

- Uncommunicative
- Argumentative
- Threatens to leave the Association
- Blatantly violates policies
- Will not file requested information
- Makes unreasonable financial demands

Ramifications of Weak Chapter Relationships:

- Frustration and bad feelings can spread across components
- Delivery of services at local level could be disrupted
- Membership retention & recruitment are negatively affected if negative impressions are made

Cecilia Sepp, CAE, ACNP
Chapter Role in Organization

I've already discussed the importance of including chapters in your organization structure and governance system. In this section I would like to expand on some of the areas where chapters have a role in moving the organization forward.

Partners – Not Competition

Often, I hear association staff say that the chapters are their competition. I shake my head when I hear this and recall what a former supervisor of mine used to say, "You need an attitude adjustment."

If you are looking at your chapters as competition, you are setting yourself up for a bad relationship. If your chapter network is established to support the activities of the organization and you are using your chapter network as a delivery vehicle for services and information, then you are both sharing in success. Any revenue, value, or good feelings generated is shared by the entire organization.

Chapters are part of the organization, so things should flow from the national to the local level when it comes to delivering services to your members. In an ideal situation, you would be providing programming and money to the chapter to deliver services like events. If sponsorship dollars are involved, those relationship introductions can come from both the national organization and the local chapter leaders as part of an overall corporate partnership package or offering to your sponsors. Not only does it help chapters, it can increase the value of participating in a corporate partner program for the companies that want to reach your audiences. Expanding the corporate partner's reach through the chapter network is a "value add" for any program.

There is no reason to look at your chapters as competition. Your chapters are your local partners in delivering member value whether it is through education, networking events, or representing the organization in advocacy activities.

If you have lost positive control of your chapter relationships, then you do have a problem that needs to be fixed. Many of these problems are created by treating the chapters like they are the problem. I say remember what Jesus of Nazareth said: "Take the plank out of your own eye before removing the splinter from your neighbor's." If there is an issue with your chapter relationships, it usually starts at the national level. Be aware of that and don't let the relationships sour.

Ambassador With Portfolio!

Chapters are your best ambassadors for communicating value to current and potential members. If anyone knows the benefits and value of belonging it would be somebody who is part of an active local chapter that receives support from national. If you have a strong relationship between national and chapters, they will tell people about it. This is the benefit of seeing chapters as an integral part of the organization's structure.

This offers another opportunity for local members to get involved in the organization by serving as an organizational ambassador. They can speak with members who didn't renew and encourage them to join again; they are your best resource for communicating with people who have never been a member to explain to them why membership is beneficial.

People who have a positive experience with your organization will tell others why they should be part of that experience. Think about a restaurant you really like that has great service and good food. You tell your friends and your neighbors about it so they can try it too. Having a healthy relationship with local chapters will create unofficial organizational ambassadors. If they are having a good time and getting value out of their membership experience, they will tell other people in the profession or industry about it.

Harness this energy to improve not just retention but recruitment. The best spokesman for anything is someone who has had a positive experience whether it's a membership or a product. This is why people love to read Amazon.com reviews; it gives them guidance on a product and if it will be a good fit for them. Let your chapters do the same for your association.

Provide them with information and messaging to promote the organization and why others should join, but also encourage them to add their own unique experiences and examples. Giving this support to spread the word creates Ambassadors, enhances your organization's reputation, and opens up micro-volunteering opportunities.

People will start to think, "Hey, this must be a good group if so many people are talking about how much they like it."

National Leadership Pipeline

We cannot overlook how chapters can help us fill our national leadership pipeline. Most associations have term limits for all levels of participation, whether committees or the board of directors. Thinking ahead, we will always need to have a way to find the leaders who will be next. Seeing who is involved locally and how well they do in those roles gives us an idea of how they might perform in a bigger role on the national stage.

As much as I think it is time for our chapter model to change and get away from the mini-me model, one benefit of it is you can see how people perform within that structure. If they are a good chapter board member, there's a strong probability they will be a good national board member.

Associations are always on the lookout for younger members or newer members to serve on committees, special interest groups, task forces or working groups. Your chapter leadership council is a great mechanism for identifying some of these other types of volunteers – you can ask your local chapter presidents who they see contributing and performing well in the local environment.

When you identify a potential newer volunteer, you can have a conversation with them about their interest level in future roles. If you have a leadership development program in place you can ask them if they would like to participate in it. You can get them thinking like an emotionally mature leader and give them information along the way so that when they do get to the national level, they are more than prepared to step in and lead.

Other Thoughts on the Chapter Role

Chapters bring the national organization experience home. It is a more tangible expression of an intangible relationship. **I use these words tangible and intangible because the member experience has always been a virtual one in a national organization**. Members do not see the national office every day nor do they go to a conference every day or every week or even every month. National involvement has always been via phone call, e-mail, letter, or now online.

Because of the nature of membership in national organizations, chapters are powerful allies in an increasingly noisy and segmented world. Strong relationships with them will improve the member experience, support organizational goals, and increase the positive perception of your organization.

Cecilia Sepp, CAE, ACNP
Subordinate in the IRS Code and the Group Tax Exemption

The word subordinate has a negative connotation when it comes to chapter relations – people become offended and righteously indignant for no good reason. This attitude is wrong and causes arguments that are not necessary.

I share this because – and I wish I were making this up – I was co-presenting on chapter relations at a local networking group years ago, and we used the word subordinate in relation to chapters. The entire room erupted with righteous indignation over "making Chapters subordinate like slaves" and not showing them respect as an equal. Some people even said we were being condescending.

They droned on for over 20 minutes before we could get control of the conversation again. Such a judgmental audience -- and a demonstration of a lack of understanding of the IRS Code and how it defines our organizations.

Once we reeled it back in, we realized we wasted valuable time that could have been spent on the content we were trying to present. **This is another example of why we all need to be schooled in the language of our profession.** Nonprofit management is governed by the IRS Code, specifically the sections on 501c organizations. Understanding these terms, what they mean, and why we use them is crucial to implementing programs and services correctly and legally.

The IRS has a publication that you can download that provides information about subordinate organizations within the IRS Code. This document supports the group tax exemption option that nonprofits can use for filing their 990 forms every year. Again, this is a very important task and responsibility that we need to fulfill every year whether we have chapters or not. So, if we do have chapters and we do want to have a group tax exemption, *we need to understand what subordinate actually means.*

This definition is directly from that IRS document that I have referenced[5]:

What are central and subordinate organizations?

Groups of organizations with group exemption letters have a "head" or main organization, referred to as a central organization. The central organization generally supervises or controls many chapters, called subordinate organizations. The subordinate organizations typically have similar structures, purposes and activities.

While in this book I have been using the term national organization because that is the type of group that usually has chapters, the IRS calls it the central organization. That is likely a better description, as the work flows from the top down to the chapters. Some people in our profession will still use the term parent organization but others find that offensive. After all, the chapters are not children; they're run by adults.

If we read further in this information from the IRS, we see that they note the central organization supervises or controls chapters called subordinate organizations. This is key to understanding the term subordinate. It is just their term for chapters.

Working on Group Exemptions is detailed and time consuming, but as the IRS says, "it's an administrative convenience" for all parties. To participate in a group exemption, each organization (central and all subordinates) must have an Employer Identification Number (EIN). *This does not mean that your chapters need to separately incorporate*:

---

[5] IRS Publication 4573 (Rev. 10-2019). www.irs.gov Group Exemptions

"A subordinate organization does not need to be incorporated, but it must have an organizing document and an EIN. Foreign organizations, private foundations, qualified nonprofit health insurance issuers, and Type III supporting organizations cannot qualify as subordinates."

This comes from the Davis Law Group website, where they explain group exemptions in a great online article. [6]

Why am I talking about all this? While I have several letters after my name, none of them are JD, but I have gotten into more than one argument about this very issue with my colleagues. The reason there is confusion about this is frankly we are not all attorneys. I was fortunate to learn this information about group tax exemptions early in my career because I did work with a chapter network where we had a group exemption. Unfortunately, being human beings, we tend to repeat things that are not 100% accurate. This is why I get into arguments with people, because I know you don't have to incorporate to have an EIN if you are a chapter that's part of a group exemption.

Is it a good idea to encourage your chapters to incorporate separately? My opinion – **and this is just my opinion** – it is *not* a good idea. While it does provide certain legal protections to your local volunteer leadership because they are an incorporated entity, I think it sows confusion and creates more problems than it solves.

Part of the reason people do this is the misunderstanding about when you need an EIN and how you can get one. The other motivation is a good one, which is to protect your volunteer leaders, but again it's not necessary. One way to protect your local chapter leaders if they are not incorporated is to invest in directors and

---

[6] https://www.dlgva.com/what-to-know-about-group-tax-exemptions/

officers liability insurance that covers all your volunteers and not just the board of directors.

Many times, the response I hear when I suggest expanding your directors and officers liability insurance to cover everyone is this: it's way too expensive. Yes, this makes the insurance more expensive, but can you afford the cost of driving a wedge between you and your local members?

Is it too expensive, since the protection provides clarity and better focuses staff time and resources? This is a question your individual organization needs to ask itself and answer.

Consider another perspective: This approach to incorporation at the chapter level is a leftover from the 19th and early 20th centuries, the time when these chapters were pretty much on their own and left to their own devices. Your attorney will tell you that they should incorporate for a lot of different reasons because that is their job to point this out. However, if you incorporate your chapters, they become more like affiliates because they are then separate organizations. Encouraging them to incorporate as separate entities makes them AFFILIATES and that does create competition. You also get the bonus problem of creating governance issues.

This gives your chapters the option of going out on their own, which is not the goal of any chapter program.

The goal of chapter programs is to bring people together locally throughout the year and have another avenue for delivering service from the organization. It is not to create a system of competitors that will eventually figure out they are separately incorporated, and they don't necessarily need to listen to the national organization or follow the guidelines.

In all my years working in nonprofit management and specifically with associations and chapters, I have seen these misconceptions get passed on and on and on. We are in an era where it's just not necessary anymore. While we must always protect the organization from liability, doing it the way we have been doing it is not always the best way.

Ask yourself this question when it comes to your chapter network: Should my members be spending their volunteer time staying tax exempt or should they be spending their time getting the benefit and value out of their organizational membership?

Cecilia Sepp, CAE, ACNP
Chapter Relationship Building and Management

We have a very old joke in association management: I could get so much work done if it weren't for these pesky members.

With all the tasks and deadlines that we must face as association staff, it is easy to get annoyed when we are interrupted. But if we take a step back and think about why we have all these tasks to do and why we have all these deadlines to meet, it is because we are here to serve our members. **If we forget this, we have failed.**

As I have mentioned, I often hear chapter relations professionals complaining that they can't control their chapters or that the chapters won't do what they're told. Based on my experience, this is an abdication of your responsibility to deliver a positive member experience and support a strong chapter network. This means the Chapter Relations Professional has failed, not the chapters.

Chapters do not want to be told; they want to be asked. They have every right to have that attitude because they are members of the organization. While they might be participating through a local chapter, they are first and foremost dues paying members. Overlooking the individual aspect of chapters is foolhardy.

One of the reasons I was a successful chapter relations professional is because I took the time to build and manage relationships at the local level. If you do not have a relationship of trust and transparency with your chapter leaders, you will be in a constant state of struggle that is wasteful and unnecessary.

If you do not have the temperament to manage relationships with a wide variety of individuals, you should focus on a different aspect of association management.

It is a false argument that you do not have time for this. The reason I find this a false argument is because everyone seems to have time to clean up the messes that this attitude causes. As Benjamin Franklin said, "An ounce of prevention is worth a pound of cure." You will always be better off spending time on the front end setting up a positive relationship and strong communications rather than trying to overcome anger, frustration and negativity. **There is no one more determined to complain than the person who feels ignored and overlooked.** This applies to chapters uniquely and specifically.

Often a chapter relations team is a team of one person. This does create a stressful situation for the staff person, as they not only have to do relationship management, but they have to do everything else as well. However, I will state this for your consideration: Your number one job is building those relationships. That's why you're there. You are also an important liaison between the chapters and the national organization because you can present their questions, share input and advocate for their needs.

Communicating to build and manage relationships is obnoxiously easy and you already have the tools to do it: telephone, email, and time. Take time to make phone calls and have real time conversations with individual chapter leaders. These calls don't have to go on for hours but even spending 15 or 20 minutes talking with someone gives you a lot of insights that a survey will not. If the person you are trying to reach cannot have a phone conversation, send them an e-mail and ask them how things are going. It may take them a while to get back to you but they will. On your end, be responsive even if the answer is, "I'll get back to you." Your chapter leaders need to know you take their concerns seriously and regular communication supports that message.

The other relationships you have to build and manage are the internal staff relationships. Associations have come a long way in their effort to remove silos from their organizations but we all know they are still there. In my experience it is most challenging explaining to your colleagues and coworkers what chapters are and how they fit into the work of the association. There is little or no cross-functional training when it comes to chapters, so you need to be your own best advocate and educate the rest of the staff about what you do and why you do it.

There are many opportunities for the chapter relations professional to improve the experience of the chapters and the members by working with other departments within the association. For example, if there is a local chapter where your next annual conference is being held, then you should connect that chapter with your meetings department. Sounds like a no brainer, doesn't it? But you would be surprised how many meetings departments don't think about it because they're busy planning all the other aspects of the conference. You stepping up and offering to make those introductions and build that cooperation will be much appreciated by everyone involved.

An additional challenge the chapter relations professional has is getting past a dismissive attitude from colleagues. They may not see chapters as important because they don't understand them. Therefore, they may see your work as unimportant and unrelated to anything that they are doing. You may even be called a glad hander, as I was once. The best way to overcome this is to have conversations with your coworkers and explain to them what you do and why you do it and how your department could partner with their department for better outcomes.

You may have a chief staff executive who has a very negative opinion of your chapter network. Sadly, this is not an unusual situation and I have found myself in it more than once. It is a fine line to walk between working with your chapter leaders and working with your chief staff executive in this situation. Keep the lines of communication open between you and the chief staff executive so they can see the benefits of having a chapter network. It may take time to win them over, but it can be done, so don't give up. Show the chief staff executive examples of how chapters support the organization and strengthen it. Like presenting a budget for a new program or service, use data to support your position.

Don't just make the time to build relationships; *take the time to build relationships*. "Taking the time" is a thoughtful, sincere approach to learning how you can best work together and increase the value of the member experience from the local level to the national level. It's not just about enforcing the guidelines or emailing information; it's about getting to know people.

Cecilia Sepp, CAE, ACNP

Chapter Models: Bylaws and Boards and Bank Accounts

In a previous section, I outlined the argument that the mini-me structure of chapters needs to be done away with in favor of a more agile, modern system based on the way we live now.

The min -me model relies heavily on modeling locally what is done at the national level: bylaws, boards and bank accounts. This model requires volunteers to act as unpaid Association Management Companies (AMCs) for their chapter rather than enjoying the experience. On the national staff side, a lot of staff energy and time is spent "chasing compliance." What a waste of mental and emotional energy.

Associations need to decide what should come next and how the chapter model could be reconfigured. It is crucial to promote evolution in chapters and local networking options to survive in an increasingly noisy world that offers smaller and smaller niche groups for connection and self-identification. The long-term goal of any chapter system should be to create and support a better experience for members and local volunteers.

However, making things easier for chapters makes lawyers nervous and uncomfortable. Of course, a lot of a lawyer's job is being nervous and uncomfortable because they are looking for dangerous situations that could open their clients to liability.

This doesn't mean that you can't review and streamline your chapter system, especially if you have subordinate chapters.

Let's face it: chapters are not a requirement, and some associations have eliminated chapters or chosen not to establish them. These groups go on to lead happy, productive lives, finding other ways to deliver local value or just worrying about delivering on the national level.

Let's look at it from the "clean slate" perspective: what if you didn't have chapters at all? How would you support local engagement for your members? What would that system look like? Where and how would resources be used?

When reviewing your system, keep in mind that an affiliate is not the same as a chapter, despite the bad habit in the nonprofit community of using these words interchangeably. Affiliates are stand-alone organizations that enter into an agreement with your association to support the same goals. They are not chapters. Please stop calling them that!

A concept I developed years ago when I was a Chief Staff Executive at a small professional society was called Networking Hubs. Inspired by special interest groups (SIGs), I applied the same model to local networking. Rather than having chapters with all the compliance issues like bylaws, boards, and bank accounts, we experimented with supporting members who volunteered to organize events for their fellow members. We produced the contact list, used the list to send the messages about the event, communicated with the event organizer about what to consider for planning, and promoted it in our national communication vehicles. We supported their success without redirecting resources to a local subordinate. There was nothing for the lawyers to get upset about because we controlled the privacy of the members on the contact list and no contracts were signed.

No committees were organized, no local board had to approve anything, and no reports were required.

Taking the weight of responsibility away from local volunteers did not diminish the goal of networking, learning, and building value for membership. **What it did do is create an opportunity to relieve the stress that can be created by legal liability concerns and find** ways to serve our members locally without a lot of governance compliance issues.

While this requires the national or parent organization to carry the burden of responsibility and possibly liability, *the parent organization does that anyway*. Chapters are great in many ways, but they also can be a doorway to liability that you don't control, like contracts signed by local volunteers that you don't get to review, financial misconduct, slip and fall issues at local events, and lawsuits against local boards. If they are a chapter, anything at the local level can lead right back to national for accountability. **Despite not having anything to do with the local management decisions, your association can still be liable because of the subordinate relationship.**

Removing chapters as we have known them gives oversight of the program back to the staff that manages it and relieves the burden on local volunteers. It can also protect the national association from liability by giving it back the ability to manage the local activities for the volunteers while protecting everyone from potential lawsuits or legal liability.

While this sounds nice, and I've worked for a few bosses that wanted to "get rid of the chapters" because they drove them crazy, your association likely will keep them for now. Any chapter program can improve and provide great service but it takes the commitment of staff to work with the volunteers to find what's best for YOUR network. Don't worry about what everyone else is doing. Do what works for your association and its chapters. To keep the program going in a positive direction, you need to constantly assess the current state of your chapter network. This relates directly to the health of your relationships. Review the Chapter Relations Checklist shared earlier in this book.

Association Chapter Systems: From Frustrating to Fruitful

Cecilia Sepp, CAE, ACNP
The Affiliate Issue – They are NOT Chapters!

Too often I hear members of our profession use the words chapter and affiliate interchangeably. **This is not just inaccurate; it is plain WRONG**. Because this linguistic habit lingers, confusion in this area continues, and it can cause a lot of stress for people studying for the Certified Association Executive (CAE) Exam because the study materials do this too.

Clarity Moment: Chapters and Affiliates are NOT the same thing, yet too many people in our profession use these interchangeably. Here I share a short mnemonic to help keep this straight:

Chapters are **PART** of the organization; **Affiliates** are **PARTNERS** with the organization.

Chapters are actually defined in the IRS Code as subordinate sections of a larger organization. Don't get hung up on being offended by the word subordinate – that is misplaced indignation and a lack of understanding of legal language and what words actually mean.

Take this Lesson with You: Learn the language of your profession and make sure you are fluent. It will save you a lot of time and headaches.

In this context, a subordinate is like a subsidiary; if you called chapters subsidiaries, for some reason nobody would be offended. But I guess if you are the argumentative type, you might split the hairs of how subsidiaries are more like for-profit structures. **Stop distracting yourself and focus on the situation**. Chapters are part of the organization. If the national association closes down, the Chapters go with it.

Getting an Employer Identification Number (EIN) does not incorporate an organization; that is merely an identifier for tax purposes. Often people don't understand this and get really confused. Now, you can ask your chapters to get their own incorporation status in their state to offer legal protection to their volunteer leaders, but again, this does not make them a separate 501(c) entity. State non-stock (nonprofit) status does not convey the same privileges or responsibilities as a 501(c) at the federal level.

If you are working with a local or state group that exists on its own, has its own 501(c) status, and can continue to exist with or without your organization, **that group is an affiliate.**

Agreeing to partner with these groups is great because you can share resources and promote each other's mission. Keep in mind that if you work with an affiliate, it is a group that is in your profession or industry, so you will have a lot in common.

However, you will have an agreement with an affiliate similar to a contract. Since they aren't chapters, you do not have the same level of authority and control over the activities of an affiliate. They are definitely equal partners whether or not you let them use your logo and let them SAY they are a chapter.

Keeping this language clear makes your life and the organization's work much easier. You can also create a new term for this type of partnership to make it even clearer how your relationship works and how it fits – or doesn't – into your governance system.

An excellent example is a client I worked with a few years ago on their Chapter Leadership Manual. During the process, I learned that their "chapters" were not really chapters; they were affiliates. We talked through how their system was set up and how the affiliates were separate organizations. This was making things murky, but we had to work within the communication and marketing of this program. We developed the term "affiliated chapters" to show that the groups were part of the program but not traditional chapters.

Your organization can do that too! Don't be trapped by language or what other organizations are doing. As Jamie Notter and Maddie Grant wrote in their book, *Humanize,* "sometimes a 'best practice' isn't best – it's just what everyone else is doing."

Cecilia Sepp, CAE, ACNP

Chapters or Affiliates: Comanches or Mongols?

As I mentioned earlier, the terms chapters and affiliates are used interchangeably and totally incorrectly. These are completely different entities, and if they're incorporated into your governance structure, they need to be incorporated correctly. The inaccurate and incorrect use of these terms often causes confusion and turmoil for those trying to understand and manage a system, so let's use some historic examples to clear this up a bit.

Years ago, I was doing a lot of reading about Genghis Khan and the Mongol empire. Right about the same time I was doing a lot of reading about Comancheria, which was the empire of the Comanche tribe of North America. While most of us have heard of Genghis Khan I would make a guess that many of us have not heard of Comancheria or even knew it existed.

Comancheria was a broad area and included a large chunk of what is now considered the southwestern United States. This is where the Comanches roamed and lived a nomadic lifestyle very similar to the Mongols of the Asian steppes.

These two groups have a lot in common, yet in the end they're completely different. It's why I think it's a good comparison when we are comparing chapters and affiliates, and it's also a little more fun than the legalese!

Let's start with what they have in common:
1. both Mongols and Comanches are nomadic tribes
2. both Mongols and Comanches dominated their regions because they adopted horseback riding (and horseback warfare) before other tribes around them
3. both lived off the land, gathering resources such as food, water and supplies from the environment around them

Association Chapter Systems: From Frustrating to Fruitful

4. both incorporated individuals from outside their group to join it and make it stronger
5. both made war on the people around them in order to maintain their dominance
6. both were feared for good reason; they were excellent warriors and built scary reputations

Now let's talk about how they are different:

1. Mongols had a unified empire under one ruling government
2. Comanches did not have a unified government of any kind
3. Mongols created an internal infrastructure where they could implement laws and enforce them, as well as an empire-wide communication system
4. Comanches might reach out to each other and work together on an ad hoc basis but then they would go their separate ways
5. A treaty with one Comanche tribe did not extend to the other tribes. The US Government learned that the hard way.
6. Mongols dominated most of Asia because of their unity.
7. Comanches did not dominate the entire continent of North America; they could only dominate one section of it because they were a loose confederation of different tribes

The question to ask yourself when looking at your chapter network or system is this: am I working with Mongols or Comanches?

After reading these lists I've created, you've probably already figured out that Mongols are chapters and Comanches are affiliates. Why is that?

Mongols were unified across a large section of Asia with a top-down government. While their empire was vast and covered many different areas they shared a common goal, common laws, and a common communication system which was very similar to what was called the Pony Express in early United States history.

When looking at actual chapters which are part of the organization, they are part of a larger whole, which makes chapters Mongols.

Comanches, on the other hand, are more similar to the Celtic tribes of Europe. In both cases many groups of people identified using the same term, whether Comanche or Celt, but they never unified under one banner or one government long enough to have an impact. It eventually led to their downfall.

That doesn't mean affiliates are going to fail. What Comanches represent in this example is a loose confederation working together because they are similar but not the same.

Affiliates are organizations that stand on their own but may work with your organization toward a common goal because you are similar – but you are not the same.

This is where the danger of using language inaccurately comes in for any organization. If you are actually working with affiliates and trying to treat them like chapters, you are going to have legal issues as well as relationship management issues. Both of these can be avoided by having a clear understanding of what sort of a system you're working with.

You cannot enforce the same type of guidelines or requirements on an affiliate that you can ask of a chapter unless it is completely spelled out in your affiliate contract. Chapter guidelines are more easily enforceable because the chapter is already part of your organization and is most likely receiving support and services from it.

Integrating chapters into your governance system also incorporates them into your leadership funnel. Affiliates may not have that opportunity based on the type of relationship you create and the agreement that is signed. In some ways, chapters have more opportunities within the organization than a true affiliate because they can get involved in leadership more easily and help shape the future of the organization.

You may not decide to extend that opportunity to an affiliate because they are your competition in the long run. You may be hesitant to let them into the top tiers of the organization because you could be sharing vital information.

An affiliate is a partner with your organization and may be allowed to call themselves a chapter of the organization and use the logo but they can walk away after the agreement ends. They don't need to renew it because they are a separate organization.

Relationship management with affiliated organizations Is much different than with chapters because you cannot tell – you need to ask. Despite having an agreement with an affiliated organization, you can only control what is in the contract.

In my experience, I have found you can avoid a lot of wasted time, bad feelings, and poorly used resources by making sure your system is set up to work whether it's a chapter or an affiliate. When these words are used interchangeably and not applied accurately, we make wrong choices and poor decisions.

That's why you have to ask yourself: am I working with Mongols or Comanches?

Here's a great place to remind you of an important distinction when answering that question:

Chapters are PART OF the organization.

Affiliates are PARTNERS WITH the organization.

Cecilia Sepp, CAE, ACNP
Chapter Guidelines

Creating chapters involves having a system with an application process, requirements to become a chapter, and expectations for performance when approved as a chapter. These expectations are often called chapter guidelines.

As I have already mentioned, setting volunteer expectations is key to success for the volunteer and for the organization. **We do have to keep in mind that guidelines are not bylaws.** What I mean by this is they do not have the same level of legal gravitas nor should they. Guidelines do not have the same weight as a contract or any other legal document; what they do is outline expectations.

Where I see chapter programs get into trouble is when they treat the chapter guidelines as if they are some sort of a legally binding contract. That's not what they are although many chapter relations professionals would like them to be. I say that because there is a certain level of frustration when working with chapters that are not fulfilling their end of the bargain. Keep in mind that members who volunteer to run local chapters are not unpaid employees – we need to make sure that the guidelines are not onerous or draconian.

A good way to approach your chapter guidelines is this: They are not handcuffs. Now you might be a chapter relations professional reading this and getting a little annoyed by this attitude. I understand that because it can be frustrating working with local leaders who are not fulfilling all of the expectations you have set for them – and somewhere along the line agreed to do. But I learned from my many years as a chapter relations professional that we need to have flexibility in our approach to managing chapter guidelines because these are volunteers. We can't expect them to put in hours and hours every week; volunteers do this in their "spare time" outside of their jobs and other responsibilities.

While there should be an expectation of performance, especially if you are giving them rebate money, when looking at any chapter network, you are going to see varied sizes, budgets, available volunteer hours, and sometimes part-time staff. You cannot expect the same level of performance from every chapter because they are all going to have different resources.

This is why I highly recommend when you are creating chapter guidelines that they be minimal guidelines, similar to industry standards. If you do research using American Society of Association Executives (ASAE) materials and resources on why we have industry standards and what they should do, industry standards need to be minimal so that all members in that industry can comply with them. Taking this approach with chapter guidelines will help support better outcomes.

So, what should be in chapter guidelines? Here are some suggestions that are fairly common:

- event activity – you might ask that they hold two to three in-person events every year
- online activity – you might ask that they hold six online webinars each year
- communications – you might ask that they communicate with their chapter members once a month to update them on any local or national news
- regular reporting to national – this could be financial activity, event activity or any other item you want to track (yes, I understand the irony that I push back on reporting but it's a common approach to guidelines creation and tracking. Just make sure it's easy to do!!)

If you are using what I call the "mini-me" chapter structure, in your guidelines you might ask that they have bylaws, a board of directors, succession plans, and a committee structure. As I noted earlier, this structure is outdated and from another era. The way we live now does not require this type of structure because we have much faster ways of communicating and we can use technology for better coordination with our chapters.

We still see in the industry that we have a process for chapter recognition that requires all these things. But we don't have to keep doing this.

If you are looking to revamp your chapter structure, reviewing your guidelines is a great place to start. This is where you can change your expectations and make it easier for your volunteers to make things happen. It's also a jumping-off point for reviewing your required chapter structure and creating one that is modern and adapted to the way we live in the 21st century.

Whatever you put in your chapter guidelines, because again this will depend on your structure at your organization, **they should never be used as a weapon to beat your chapters down**. That is not why you have chapter guidelines and it's not how they should be used. I have seen too many organizations creating draconian systems that are more about control than outcomes. Guidelines are meant to encourage activity and deliver member value at the local level. That's it.

Guidelines can also be a measurement of chapter health. You can use these to find chapters that are struggling to deliver services to the local members; this gives you an opportunity to start a conversation about what kind of help they might need to improve their performance. If you see a chapter that used to regularly report activities that is not reporting as often, or the reports have nothing to show for that quarter, that's a warning sign.

Chapter guidelines should be used as a tool for setting expectations and giving local chapters direction. For the national organization, it is a mechanism for measuring delivery of member services. An important aspect of this mechanism is letting chapters help create them and then update them as needed. As Cheryl Ronk, CAE, FASAE, says, "People support that which they help create." Regular chapter guideline review and updating is an excellent way to get buy-in into the program and increased support of the organization's mission.

Chapter guidelines should support resources being sent directly to the members where they live and work. They should not be seen as binding contracts, bylaws, or legal documents of any kind. Remember: subordinate chapters are part of the organization, not separate entities. If they were separate entities, which we would call an affiliate, then you would have a contract situation.

Chapter Guidelines support the work of our volunteer leaders locally and help deliver value to our members. They also help you create stronger relationships with your local chapters and build a stronger network. Make sure they are clear, doable, and measurable – just like SMART goals.

Cecilia Sepp, CAE, ACNP

Rogue Chapters

Rogue Chapters is a topic I see pop up in discussions within the association community. It is usually meant in a negative way and relates directly to a lack of control over the chapters by the national organization staff. I think people say this out of frustration more than anything else, but we need to find out why the chapter is behaving badly.

First of all, the concept of "rogue" has changed over the years. Originally, a rogue was a bad person who did bad things. Their actions broke rules or did a lot of damage – think highwaymen or outlaws. However, "going rogue" also means (according to Merriam-Webster Dictionary) in the modern sense of the word, *"to begin to behave in an independent or uncontrolled way that is not authorized, normal, or expected."*

Now, behaving in unexpected ways is not always a bad thing because sometimes going rogue can solve a problem, diffuse a serious situation, or present an imaginative alternative. **Acting independently might be "going rogue" because it is outside of the norms that have been set.**

A perfect example is my company name, Rogue Tulips Consulting, which came from finding tulips growing in the front lawn rather than in the garden bed where they originated. In this sense, the tulips were rogue for doing the unexpected and blooming outside the box. (Yes, it *is* a nice tie-in to our tagline.)

When it comes to chapters going rogue, we need to address our own control issues. That's right: many times, **we are exasperated with our chapters because we feel back at national that we are losing control of the situation**. Therefore, the chapters must be doing something wrong because they aren't doing what we tell them, and they are not behaving in an expected and acceptable way.

Once we address our own control issues and remember that we are seeking collaboration and partnership rather than control, it helps us evaluate what is happening and how to improve the situation. **There are times that chapters do something that seems "roguish" when they just don't know any better.** For example, logo abuse seems to be a frequent issue among chapters. They use it incorrectly, take it apart and add things to it, or just ignore it and create their own.

Issues like that can be addressed through information and education; usually an honest and open discussion that begins with a question – "Why did you put the Gateway arch in the middle of the logo?" – leads to clarity and supports building relationships. **Often you will find that no harm was intended; it was just misdirected enthusiasm.**

On the other hand, we need to seriously address the issue of INTENT. **Yes, there are chapter leaders who intentionally act out and cause disruption within the organization.** This can be driven by a variety of reasons, but they all come back to the individual's issues. Individuals who instigate and aggravate tense situations act this way because (1) they are angry that they have been overlooked by the organization; (2) they are angry about a new guideline; (3) they are angry that you aren't taking their chapter seriously enough; (4) they are angry you are not taking THEM (the individual) seriously enough.

In my long experience working with chapters, bad behavior happens when people are angry. It could be gradations of anger (insulted, annoyed, frustrated) **but it still comes back to someone**

who is upset about something and you need to figure out what it is.

If you have ever had a chapter threaten to leave the organization ("we don't need you – we can do what we do alone"), that is usually a cry for attention, which means you have been ignoring this particular chapter or they FEEL you have been ignoring them. Find out what is really bothering them; did they think they should have won a chapter award? Did you overlook them as a case study in the newsletter about high-performing chapters? Did they suggest an idea that you didn't pursue?

Don't assume one loud angry voice in your chapter speaks for everyone. Talk to more than one person about the situation and what is driving it. **While you may think from a distance that your chapters are laughing at you, saying "nyah nyah nyah MAKE ME," or reveling in their disobedience, what they are really trying to do is get your attention.**

Whatever the reason for your chapters' roguish behavior, I have found over the years that people don't get angry or upset unless they care. Start from that place of inquiry, using beginner's mind[7], and you will find an opportunity to build even stronger relationships with your chapters.

---

[7] Beginner's Mind: **Shoshin** (Japanese: 初心) is a concept from Zen Buddhism meaning **beginner's mind**. It refers to having an attitude of openness, eagerness, and lack of preconceptions when studying, even at an advanced level, just as a beginner would. From Wikipedia https://en.wikipedia.org/wiki/Shoshin

Cecilia Sepp, CAE, ACNP
Tracking Chapter Bank Accounts

Chapter bank accounts have been the bane of many a chapter relations professional's existence. Knowing how much money chapters have is why we ask them to do financial reports. But sometimes we don't know where that money is and this can lead to problems like embezzlement. Another issue that we can find with local chapter bank accounts is that we don't know who the signatories are and it's not possible to work with the bank to get that money back or transfer it to new leadership.

Another fun issue with chapter bank accounts is when the people who are the signatories retire, move, die, or change careers. Sometimes they just take off and they don't look back. They don't even think about giving that money back or making sure it is accessible.

Many associations take a hands-off approach and attitude toward chapter bank accounts. This is a mistake. That money does not belong to the chapter; that money belongs to the members. If that money comes from rebates, you can make the argument that it belongs to the national association. In my opinion, the best attitude to take is this money belongs to the members and that is why the national association gave it to the chapters, so that it could be used locally.

This is another issue where I hear people say they don't have time to deal with it. Here's a rude awakening: The National association is responsible and accountable for how funds are used. In a subordinate chapter situation, which is what this book is about, you had better find the time to manage these chapter bank accounts.

Too often volunteer leaders leave the money sitting in the bank because they don't want to be the one to use it. It piles up and delivers nothing of value to anyone. This is why the association should set up their chapter support system to include sharing the financial information. If possible, you may also want to have someone from the national staff on the account so that money can be accessed should the chapter be dissolved or the local leadership disappears.

This is not something that associations tend to think about when setting up their chapters. If you have chapter guidelines, this should be one of the expectations within those chapter guidelines. Even if chapters bring in their own income from local events, that money still belongs to the members and therefore should be accessible by the National association if necessary.

Over my career I have seen many examples of chapter embezzlement because the National association had no mechanism in place for tracking chapter finances. Asking for a quarterly financial report is all well and good, but if you don't have a way to find that money and track it, the report becomes meaningless. While associations may have a mechanism in place to dissolve a local chapter that includes returning any funds that have not been used, this does not address the issue of chapters that become dormant and there is no local contact person.

Chapters having their own funds is great if those funds are being used. **However, I have come to the opinion that chapters should not have their own bank accounts and funds.** The National association should have a chapter fund that supports their local activities. This might sound radical since we are still stuck in our old thinking on the chapter model but money that sits in a bank and is unused or inaccessible does no one any good.

For chapter funds to be used well and responsibly, our chapter training would have to include internal financial controls. **While we might talk about budgets for chapters, I don't think we talk enough about responsible money management for chapters.** We should also educate them about audits if we are going to let them have this money and use it. Quarterly financial reports will not give you the insight that an annual audit does. While our chapter leaders are volunteers and we all love volunteers, by taking on that role as a volunteer leader, they become accountable and responsible.

As a profession we need to ask ourselves: **Is it fair to put this financial burden on a chapter leader when they will legally be liable?** The follow-up question is: Are our chapter leaders included in our Directors & Officers (D&O) liability insurance? The next question: Do we want to place our national leadership in a situation where they are liable for misappropriated funds? I'm sure the lawyers love this paragraph – it's all about liability.

Another thing to consider are escheat laws, which exist in all 50 states, the District of Columbia, and Puerto Rico; this allows state governments to confiscate bank accounts considered abandoned because they have been dormant. These are considered unclaimed property and unless you can act on the account, the state will take the money. We shouldn't allow our members' money to go to someone else.

If your chapters have their own bank accounts, here's some of the information you should have:

- Name of the bank where the account is
- Names of the signatories on the bank – and this should always be updated as leadership changes
- Copies of bank statements (include this in your quarterly financial report)
- Access to the account should the chapter dissolve
- Chapter internal controls for managing their funds
- Annual chapter audits that follow Generally Accepted Accounting Principles (GAAP)

Association Chapter Systems: From Frustrating to Fruitful

When I was in college, the most valuable lesson I learned in sociology class was this: money has no value except in exchange. Letting it sit in the bank makes it useless.

Cecilia Sepp, CAE, ACNP
Dissolving Inactive Chapters

Inactive chapters are a testament to wasted resources. Allowing a chapter that is doing nothing and contributing nothing brings down the whole organization and dampens the energy of your chapter network.

This is why having your processes and procedures in place and ready to go before this happens is essential. We are speaking specifically in this section about chapters and not affiliates because, as we already know, those are very different things.

When a chapter stops providing services at the local level, you should of course investigate and find out what is going on before you act. For example, the current chapter leadership may have given up or maybe they got new jobs and they didn't have time to focus on the chapter work. You may have declining membership in the area that the chapter serves. There may be bad feelings in this chapter – the leadership may be fighting with each other, and this turns the members off, so they disengage.

Again, this is why you need to find out what the heck is going on with your chapters.

The best place to start with investigating whether or not you dissolve a chapter is your chapter guidelines. They should outline the expected activities as well as the responsibilities that the local leadership takes on for your chapter. Reviewing whether or not they are holding events, sharing financial information, or communicating at any level with their chapter members will give you a good idea of their activity level as well as their commitment level.

For example, your guidelines might require 3 events per year. In an ideal situation, you would be on their e-mail list and know when they are doing things. They might also have to file a report with you about what activities they have done so far every year. You can access both of these resources to find out what is going on.

When it comes to communications, if you are on their e-mail list you will know if they're communicating with the members or not. These communications could be updates from national, upcoming events from the local chapter, or local news of interest to the members. If you're not seeing anything like this, it's not happening.

I have an interesting example of a chapter that needed to be dissolved from my time at the American Corporate Counsel Association (now known as the Association of Corporate Counsel) where I once served as Chapter Relations Director. We had a chapter called the Intermountain Chapter and it included several less-populated Western states including Utah, Idaho, Nevada, Montana, and Wyoming.

You might be asking yourself why there would be a chapter with such a large geographic service area and not a lot of people. When I started in this position, I asked myself the same thing. What I learned was there was a member who worked at a company that had a private jet that he could use as needed. It being such a large geographic area, when they were having an event, he would use the company's jet to fly around to every state and pick people up. As you can imagine, that made things much easier in such a broad area; but it's not sustainable at all.

When that person left the company and no longer had access to the jet, there was no other way to pull people together from such a broad area. It was difficult to get people involved and there was really no easy place for them to get together. Despite including so many states, there just weren't a lot of corporate counsel in the area and they had difficulty maintaining the minimum required membership.

A few of the people in the chapter tried very hard to keep it going but it eventually lost steam. There was just no way for this chapter to work anymore. This is a great lesson for creating your guidelines because you want to outline reasonable geographic service areas with the minimum member requirement to launch a chapter.

Eventually we convinced the people in that chapter it just couldn't work anymore. We took our time doing it because we wanted people to feel comfortable with the decision and we did not want to seem like we were coming down really hard on them. In the end there was just no way for this chapter to exist or succeed.

This is an extreme example of a dissolution situation but it does show us trends that we have to monitor with any chapter. In this example, we had an unsustainable situation because of the private jet. However, you will see other unsustainable situations in a chapter such as the same people staying on the board. This eventually leads to volunteer burnout and that's not sustainable. You may also discover a toxic chapter culture and that is driving down engagement. Again, this is not sustainable because no one wants to be involved in a bad chapter. It's just not worth their time and energy.

As we also saw in this example, you just may not have enough members in that area to be successful as a chapter. That is also unsustainable. If you don't have enough people, nobody's going to show up and you won't have enough volunteers. While you will always find valiant volunteers who are willing to continue the work, they will become incredibly discouraged and disappointed. This will influence their perception of the national organization as well because you let it go on so long.

From the staff and association's perspective, it's also not worth their time and energy. This is why you should have a code of conduct for all levels of your membership and leadership. If you have a code of conduct for your chapter leaders, you can build the case for dissolution if needed. You are not sharing the organization's valuable resources locally so they can be squandered by people who are not serious about the commitment.

When it comes to inactive chapters, you need to dissolve them for the good of the organization. The bad feelings generated from poorly performing chapters will eventually seep across your entire organization and you will see negative outcomes because of it.

Will the members in that dissolved chapter be disappointed? Yes, they probably will be, especially if it's a benefit of membership. But I would bet they would be much happier being part of a different kind of networking group that was actually active and worth their time and energy. You can always reserve the option to reboot this chapter later on if you have a membership increase locally or new people willing to take on the leadership.

Anyone who has been active as a volunteer knows how much time and energy it takes so we want to make sure that it's a good experience. When it comes to the local members of the chapter, especially if it is a member benefit, it needs to demonstrate value or it is meaningless as a benefit.

Monitoring chapter activity and outcomes is key to having a strong chapter network. Regular monitoring of activities gives you a better understanding of what is actually happening in your chapter network and whether or not you need to take action of any kind. Regular monitoring also prevents you from being blindsided when you find out something is going wrong or things are not being done. Note I say "monitoring," not reporting requirements. This means you need to be proactive in staying in touch with your chapters to find out what is happening – or not happening as the case may be.

A lack of interest and intervention by the national organization opens it to liability. A hands-off approach is not the best method when it comes to working with your chapters. Being consistently involved with your chapters and building strong relationships will prevent the dissolution of chapters by identifying the chapters that are struggling. It creates unity of purpose and an ability to move the mission of the organization forward.

Talk to your chapters; don't dictate to them. It's how you build a strong partnership.

Cecilia Sepp, CAE, ACNP
Supporting Chapters with Current Technology

A serious challenge for supporting local chapters is the issue of technology infrastructure. Another term for this is the tech stack but whichever phrase you use, it's all about what technology your chapter is using and HOW they are using it. Are they part of the national organization's tech stack? Or do they use whatever they want? And if they use whatever they want, does it talk to anyone else's tech stack?

On this topic we tend to have more questions than answers because there is no really easy solution. There are pros and cons to letting chapters build their own tech stack, just as there are pros and cons to letting them into the national tech stack. I truly believe if I could answer this question well for everyone, I would likely be able to retire because I would be so wealthy from selling the solution.

The challenges for managing chapters within your technology infrastructure are myriad.

Most association management systems (AMS) do not include a module for chapter management. While it may include fields so that you can assign chapters or tag chapter leaders, it's difficult to find an AMS that will let you actually manage each chapter individually. In an ideal world, these modules would allow the chapters to access your system to manage their local work without worrying about multiple tech stacks across your chapter network.

Your association can pay extra to have a module designed for you but this can become incredibly expensive. It also reduces the benefit of buying an AMS, which is getting an integrated system that needs very little tailoring.

This leads us to an ongoing question of what to do about local chapter technology. Do we give them access to our database? Do we give them credentials to use the national association's technology infrastructure? Do we support their choice to have their own separate website or do we give them a page on the national website?

However, every association is different and each chapter within their association is unique. We will find different levels of technological skill sets among our national staff and our local leaders. Not everyone is tech savvy and not everyone adapts to it easily. While training can always be offered, some people are just intimidated by different technologies. They are comfortable with their technology infrastructure but may not like yours.

We know that having everyone use the same technology is beneficial, but we also have to ask how we would put that in place. Which technology would we use? Would we require local chapters to give up their own technology infrastructure and use the one we recommend? Where would the funds come from to pay for the shared technology infrastructure?

As an advocate for closer ties with chapters and more support from national, my recommendation would be to find a technology infrastructure that supports the volunteer work of your local chapters and talks to your system at the national level.

This could take several different forms including:

1. An expanded license for Google Workspace, Office365 or a similar product so chapters could have access to the same tools.
2. Increased association management company (AMC) services for your chapters where national staff would manage websites, member communications, and other services supported by technology.
3. Funding the development of a chapter management module that integrates with your AMS and would provide all chapters

the same management platform for their work. A benefit of this is that national staff could see what chapters are working on and offer assistance as needed.
4. Contract with an AMC to manage your chapters – this would answer a lot of these questions.
5. There are no easy answers but a solution is out there. Conduct a tech stack audit, review the needs of your chapters, assess available resources, and ask your chapters to give you input on what they want and need.

Cecilia Sepp, CAE, ACNP
Chapter Leadership Training

When it comes to volunteer leaders at all levels, whether it's the board of directors or chapters, we all talk about the importance and the need for educating and training. But do we actually do it well?

When I pose the question, "Are we doing it well," it is about content, but it is also about frequency. Many times, because of time constraints and other pressures on staff, we tend to do it once a year. This generally has made sense in the past because at in-person events, we might hold a chapter leadership training workshop in conjunction with a larger meeting. When that was the best way to get people together, that made a lot of sense. In today's world most of us are pressed for time because technology lied to us.

Technology told us it would free up our time but that turned out not to be true. We find ourselves constantly working or constantly checking messages of all kinds because technology is demanding of our attention and in our face 24 hours per day. Technology encourages us to work more and longer hours because we are in virtual offices even if we have a brick-and-mortar space. As long as we have a device with us, we are always at work no matter where we are physically.

This 24-hour work mindset saps people's energy and their interest in doing "one more thing" in addition to work and home life. There may also be a lack of money for people to attend meetings in person or they may not get approved for time outside of the office to do a volunteer function. Since online participation has replaced in-person participation for many organizations and individuals, thus reducing those essential in-person relationship building opportunities, ties to professional associations or trade associations may not be as strong as they once were.

Relying on one in-person meeting per year to conduct chapter leadership training is no longer practical – we just don't live that way any longer.

But we do live in a world of technology that allows us to connect in real time, share resources online, and create virtual communities for ongoing learning and knowledge sharing. Using online conference tools like Zoom or Webex or Microsoft Teams allows us to bring people together from all over the world to receive training for their volunteer leadership role. It is my opinion that we overlook the power of regular online training for volunteer leaders although I'm sure some of you reading this are shaking your head and saying, "Not my organization."

Yes, your organization too.

You might be chafing a little bit at that comment and thinking, "We do online training, so we are in good shape." My questions for you are: how often are you offering the online training? Is it in real time or is it recorded? Are there digital resources available to support this online learning? Is the content of this training applicable and usable for a chapter leader? Does it provide practical steps for putting on an event? Does it teach them how to put together an e-newsletter? Does it explain to them how streamlined governance is to their benefit?

Giving them a foundation of how the organization works at the national level is important because if they're going to be part of the governance system and the organizational structure, they need to know where they fit in. Of course we want them to know what the mission statement is. Of course, we want them to know the vision of the organization and its core values. These are foundational concepts for mission fulfillment. But are these items actually teaching them how to lead the local chapter?

Are we giving them the skills they need to put together a meeting agenda? Are we explaining to them the responsibilities of being the treasurer of a local chapter? Are we teaching them how to create a budget or conduct an audit? Are we showing them how to do marketing that brings people to events?

We cannot give people a chapter leadership role without giving them the practical skills that they need. Again, teaching them the mission is great but that's not going to help them create a meeting agenda.

This is where an online digital library filled with templates and examples will support your training efforts. Don't just tell them, show them. Creating one of these libraries might sound challenging and maybe a bit overwhelming but if you encourage your local chapters to share their templates and how they do things, not only are they participating in building their own knowledge base but that saves time for national staff because they don't have to create these things. They are already out there, so find and share them.

In this section I've talked a lot about the practical aspect of what we might put into training and how we might deliver it. But we of course need to dig deeper and we need to talk about leadership training. Being a leader comes naturally to some people but others need to be taught these skills. The quality of leadership at any level determines if you will have negative outcomes or positive outcomes. In addition, it will determine if you have a chapter that works well or is in a constant state of turmoil.

Recruiting leaders thoughtfully can help avert turmoil because we need to know what kind of people we're looking for; what are the personality traits we need for success? Much of this relates directly to emotional maturity or emotional quotient (EQ). If we recruit emotionally immature people who do not understand that leadership is about others and not them, then we will have bad outcomes. This will lead to an underperforming chapter with unhappy members who may eventually give up and leave.

If we focus on finding emotionally mature leaders, it is much easier for them to understand that leadership is about other people. It doesn't matter if you are the chapter president or the chair of a committee in a local chapter – it is about serving other people and not your own agenda. In my experience we do not say this clearly enough or bluntly enough. This leads us to dealing with too many issues like people not getting along and getting in the way of progress.

If we have a leader in place who is there for the wrong reason, we are bringing turmoil and chaos on our own heads. This leads to wasted resources, negative attitudes and diminishing the member experience. Too often I see associations ignore these people and hope they will go away. They won't.

This is where leadership training can help avert this situation. An addendum to your chapter guidelines should include volunteer leader job descriptions and requirements of performance. It should include a code of conduct that is enforceable. If we cannot remove an underperforming leader then we are choosing to put our members into a bad situation that they can't get out of either. If we do not support chapter members asking for help in changing leadership we are creating former members.

Cecilia Sepp, CAE, ACNP
Chapter Leadership Councils

Councils are mechanisms for bringing people together in any organization. They're very similar to coalitions when you think about it because you're bringing together similar people with similar goals and activities. By bringing them together, you can improve outcomes by better focusing resources of time, energy, money, and knowledge.

The best reason to create a chapter leadership council is to build better ties and stronger relationships between the national organization and the local chapters. Throughout this book I have emphasized the importance of strong relationships with our volunteer leaders; this is a must in a chapter network. The goal of chapters is not competition between the local groups and national – the goal of chapters is to deliver local services for your members where they actually live and work.

Chapters are an integral part of your organization structure and governance. To reduce frustration in working with chapters and increase the fruitful outcomes we seek, we need to show them the respect they deserve. Creating a council on which all chapter presidents sit shows the respect the organization has for their part in the structure, appreciation for what they contribute, and serves as a mechanism for building cohesion.

The 21st century is set apart by technology but as far as living in an era of division and balkanization, it is not unusual. There have been many times in the past where smaller and smaller groups of people break off and people become isolated from each other. That's why in the 21st century, if you have a chapter network, you should have a chapter leadership council. It brings together people with a common purpose in support of a common mission, which is the mission of the organization.

How you structure this council will depend on how your organization is structured and what type of governance system you have in place. Some basic steps that we all should take are the following:

- one representative per chapter, whether it is the chapter president or a designee
- regular meetings of this council to build relationships and share information
- in addition to being representatives, this council should act as a think tank for the organization when developing strategy
- it is also a testing ground for your leadership funnel to identify potential candidates for future roles, whether that's on the board of directors or other groups within the organization

Any group that wants to get anything done also needs to have its own internal structure, so on a chapter leadership council, we need to have a mission statement and roles and responsibilities for its members. Setting clear expectations for any volunteer leadership role is vital, crucial, necessary, – or whatever other urgent word you want to add to it – otherwise people flail around and waste their time and energy.

Chapter leadership councils bring an additional value benefit to those serving in these roles because it gives them a deeper and broader experience within the organization. This cannot be overlooked when looking at the member value proposition. Any volunteer role needs to bring value to that person's experience and it needs to give them skills and knowledge that they can apply in other parts of their life. One of the drivers for getting into a leadership role is to get those leadership skills. **But leadership without respect is an empty vessel.**

Cecilia Sepp, CAE, ACNP

For those staff who work with chapter networks, chapter leadership councils are an important venue for creating and maintaining relationships. As we all know, nonprofit management is the relationship industry, so we need to have systems in place for staff to build and nurture those very relationships. Having a council in place where chapter representatives can communicate in a formal way with the national organization helps minimize the "us versus them" attitude that tends to develop in these networks.

If we want to have a fruitful relationship with chapters and not a frustrating one, we need to minimize the natural tension that will develop. I often explain to people that tension is not a bad thing; it is what holds things together. For example, without tension, a suspension bridge would collapse into the water. Another example: Without tension, your muscles can't work and hold you upright and support you when you walk or stand.

But when that tension becomes negative tension and starts to pull things apart, frustration sets in and relationships are damaged. If a relationship becomes one-sided and it appears one person in the relationship has all the power and influence, or it appears that one person in the relationship is not taken seriously and not heard, this is when emotions take charge. It's difficult to resolve issues when people are upset, so the best strategy is to maintain a healthy relationship so that issues can be discussed and resolved in a reasonable fashion.

An important aspect you may overlook when it comes to chapter leadership councils is this: they are a way for chapters to bring forth issues and questions from the general membership. When we consider that the people we serve are members of these chapters, we need to listen. Stop trying to control the chapters and try listening to your chapters. **It's amazing what you can learn and the positive**

outcomes you can create together when you listen and don't just hear.

I have worked with more than one chief staff executive that hated the chapters and would repeatedly comment that they would love to get rid of them. This demonstrates shortsightedness and small-mindedness, as well as forgetting why we work in associations in the first place. We are here to serve the members and to help them achieve the mission of the organization. Chapter networks are excellent ways to achieve this and integrating them into your governance structure and your organization through a chapter leadership council builds a stronger organization and helps you accomplish more than you would only from the national level.

To summarize this section, include chapter leadership councils in your governance system and your organization structure to improve relationships, better deliver services locally, and build a stronger organization overall. This increases value in membership and will help support your retention program. I often say that retention is recruitment. What I mean by this is if you have strong retention, that means you have something of value to offer and your current members will tell other people why they should join.

Everything in your organization is interconnected. Think that through when working with your chapter network and you will see some exciting results.

Cecilia Sepp, CAE, ACNP

Chapters and Strategic Planning: Work Together for Stronger Mission Impact

"Strategy without tactics is the slowest route to victory. Tactics without strategy is the noise before defeat." **Sun-Tzu, The Art of War**

501(c) organizations use the strategic planning process to assess their environment (both internal and external), to evaluate their resources, and to define issues affecting the constituency, profession or industry they represent. Ultimately, long-term goals are established that will support the mission of the organization.

Goals are the results or achievements toward which effort is directed. Put another way, goals are what you want to accomplish. This concept is well understood by most 501(c) organization management professionals, as goals are used throughout the organization in a variety of planning modes. Goals are also understood by most volunteer leaders and members, as we all use goals for measuring some aspect of our professional and/or personal lives.

Where most 501(c) organizations struggle with the process is not knowing and understanding the difference between strategy and tactics. A frequent mistake is indicating tactics as strategies, which confuses the purpose of the plan. This leads to wasted resources (time and money), lack of focus, and frustration among those implementing the plan. To develop a thoughtful strategic plan, and to fully implement it, a clear understanding of strategy and tactics must be developed first.

A goal is what you want to accomplish. A strategy is a long-term plan of action to achieve a particular goal (Wikipedia's definition). Put another way, strategy is how you will accomplish your goal. All 501(c) organization strategies should support the mission of the organization.

For example: The goal is that our 501(c) Organization will be the leading voice in our industry. A sub-goal is that we will gain an improved reputation, demonstrate increased value to our members, and find new audiences for our products and services, thus developing new revenue streams. The rationale for this goal is that we believe attaining this position will demonstrate our expertise and the superior value of our resources.

A **strategy** to accomplish this goal would be to develop a coalition among our peer organizations to lobby the federal government.

Tactics are the individual actions that, when aggregated, support strategy. According to Merriam-Webster.com, tactics are the art or skill of employing available means to accomplish an end.

These are the "what," of implementing strategy. Tactics represent the individual actions that must be conducted to implement the strategy. Successful strategic plans attach strategies and tactics to metrics and timelines for proper assessment.

For example, to support our long-term goal of becoming the leading voice in the industry, in the first quarter of the year, we will issue two white papers on industry concerns, distribute three press releases about each paper, and have six media placements (television, radio, or print) about these issues.

The strategic planning process flows from the "big picture view" (goals) to the details of implementation (tactics):

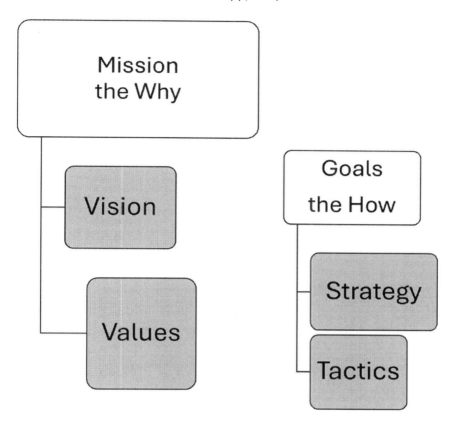

The Strategic Planning Process: How to Do It

While the age-old process of creating huge documents outlining five-year plans has fallen by the wayside, strategic planning is alive and well and essential to success. Today, modern strategic planning focuses on the discussion of strategic goals and strategies and less on exhaustive documentation of specific tactics and objectives. The planning documents are designed to improve communication and do not function as end points.

The strategic planning process of today is collaborative, innovative, and includes a broad range of stakeholders. By developing this type of process, 501(c) organizations can access the collective knowledge and experience of all segments of their community. The integration of multiple community segments into the process strengthens the organization and better supports the mission.

Leadership of Strategic Planning

There are several options for leading your strategic planning process; all are effective, but you need to choose the one that works best for your 501(c) organization.

Never forget the uniqueness of your organization when developing any sort of plan or program; create the appropriate mechanism for your structure and members.

Some common options include:

1. *The Board of Directors acts as lead with input from staff and other stakeholders.* In this scenario, the board acts as the strategic planning committee, creating and implementing the plan with mostly input from the board.
2. *Form a strategic planning committee to advise the Board of Directors.* In this scenario, the committee should have representation from all stakeholders, including board members, component leaders, staff, and other active committee volunteers who may not have an official role (such as former committee members or chapter presidents).
3. *Your 501(c) organization may choose to work with a consultant* to help guide your process, in conjunction with your strategic planning committee and staff.

No matter what option you use, the work is not done when you write the plan. Strategic planning and its implementation are part of ongoing management and operations of the 501(c) organization; the plan and its milestones should be reviewed frequently throughout the year. Continue the collaborative process with your stakeholders after the plan is put into action; a dynamic approach to strategic planning allows the organization to quickly adapt to changes in the environment or shifting resources.

Creating Context for the Strategic Planning Process

Many 5C1(c) organizations have worked hard to establish strong, member-driven institutions. Using a strategic planning process can continue to bring focus to building the 501(c) organization's understanding of stakeholders and developing systems to more fully link member needs with organizational structure and resource allocation.

In preparation for strategic planning, create context for the discussion by briefing participants on all aspects of the 501(c) organization. Briefing can be done via written materials or presentations by staff at an initial meeting.

Additionally, technology and the internet offer many venues for video or "real time" interaction. For example, a 501(c) organization can post a series of training or educational videos on YouTube, and "real time" meetings can be held using video conferencing services. By creating context for the discussions, the 501(c) organization achieves the following steps that support the strategic planning process:

- Improves leadership understanding of the relationship between mission, stakeholders, goals, strategies, and resources.
- Improves leadership focus on distinct strategic challenges or opportunities.
- Improves the ability of leadership to achieve consensus and make decisions regarding the priorities of the 501(c) organization.

- Improves the ability of leadership to communicate expectations to staff regarding strategy and metrics.

Moving on to the Planning Phase

"Prohibit seeking for omens and do away with superstitious doubts. Then, until death comes, no apparently predestined calamity need be feared." Sun-Tzu, *The Art of War*

Strategic planning can be as simple or as complex as you would like to make it. Generally, the more complex the 501(c) organization's stakeholder markets and product/service portfolio, the more complex the process will be.

Regardless of complexity, there are some common steps:

1. Discuss and agree on the process. Bring together your board of directors, staff, and other stakeholders for a meeting to discuss the goals and steps of the strategic planning process. This ensures that the primary 501(c) organization leadership is in agreement regarding how the eventual strategic plan will be created. This can be done via conference call, web session, or in person. In person is recommended for the first meeting because it is an opportunity for all to meet each other, get to know each other, and build a common understanding of what you are trying to accomplish and how. Additionally, by building understanding, stronger relationships are forged. These strong relationships are necessary to have an open and inclusive process, which requires trust, honesty, and a safe environment for open discussion.
2. Evaluate past activity: review your past strategic plan if you have one. Discuss what you liked about the plan, what worked, and what outcomes you achieved. Conversely, analyze and discuss what didn't work and why. For example, too few resources, external factors, lack of commitment to the

project or lack of time. Then ask the question: Should these "failed" times be revisited and redeployed with a better support system and action plan?
3. Pull out your mission statement: Did your previous plan support the mission? If not, why not? If yes, then note where it did this well and keep in mind when developing the next plan.
4. Discuss and identify goals: to identify a consensus on what you want the 501(c) organization to accomplish, discuss the goals for the organization.
5. When goals are agreed to, discuss how each goal applies to each segment of your 501(c) Organization. For example, how will increased membership recruitment help chapters? How will it support the knowledge base of SIGs? Are committees affected by increased recruitment numbers?
6. Now that goals are agreed to, discuss the strategy that applies to reaching that goal. For example, if a goal is to increase retention, then the strategy would be to increase perceived value of membership to current members.
7. Develop consensus on strategies to achieve goals: strategies are the primary means by which you'll achieve the goals. Strategies are used to communicate the road map for achieving the goals and are used to guide allocation of resources.

Where do Tactics Come in?

After the strategic plan is written, a work plan including tactics that support goals and strategies is written. (You might call it by another name.) The work plan indicates individual responsibility for each area, metrics for tracking progress, and milestones to keep the plan on track. This document should be used as a daily and annual guide for building a successful 501(c) organization based on goal and strategy-driven decisions.

In developing this plan, determine specific tactics linked to each strategy; there will be six to ten key tasks that are central to accomplishment. It is important in strategic planning to identify these because it helps ensure that leadership has a common understanding on how a specific strategy will be implemented.

In addition, tactics require resources, so at this point in the process, allocation must be done. Usually, this part of the strategic plan implementation is created by staff to prepare staffing and budget requirements. It is then submitted to the 501(c) organization leadership for review and approval.

"Opportunities multiply as they are seized."
Sun-Tzu, The Art of War

Using your strategic planning process to build stronger relationships with all your stakeholders is one opportunity that yields many others for your 501(c) organization. Aligning all your stakeholder and member segments to support the strategic goals of the 501(c) organization creates a stronger membership, a nimbler organization, and a committed leadership that learns to put the needs of the organization over their personal agendas.

These opportunities lead to multiple benefits, and that is a strategy worth pursuing.

Cecilia Sepp, CAE, ACNP
Recommended Resources on Strategy Development

- The Art of War by Sun-Tzu: this book is considered the definitive text on strategy. While it is focused on military aspects of strategy, his teachings can be applied to other areas.
- A Spy's Guide to Strategy by John Braddock, copyright 2017. Contact the author at www.spysguide.com
- Strategic Planning for Public and Nonprofit Organizations: A Guide to Strengthening and Sustaining Organizational Achievement (Bryson on Strategic Planning) [Hardcover] by John M. Bryson
- Strategic Planning Made Simple: 10 Easy Steps by Lori Williams

Cecilia Sepp, CAE, ACNP
Is your Chapter System Really That Bad?

There is ongoing conversation in the association community about modernizing the chapter system. It comes from a lot of areas: outdated ways of delivering services locally, governance systems that no longer serve the members, and fruitless requirements to maintain chapter or affiliate status that create unpaid staff positions for volunteers.

And don't even get me started on the mushiness of the terminology. Too many associations use chapter and affiliate interchangeably when these are two very different structures.

In the move to modernize chapter systems – which I strongly support – the human elements must be considered. People have status from volunteering. People have put in time and energy to build a local chapter. Recognition and reward systems are in place that some people are working toward earning. If these are taken away, people get upset and feel disconnected and/or insulted. ("I've put in all this work anc for WHAT?? Now you've taken it away.")

The natural tension that comes from the national-chapter relationship can make things seem worse than they actually are. It's hard to balance chapter requirements with chapter service sometimes, especially when it seems like all you do is chase reports or deal with angry volunteer leaders.

Replacing the volunteer leadership "career arc" with something else is important if it is something that members have long pursued, especially if it brings professional recognition. Encouraging members to pursue a leadership pathway is important but if you want to streamline your current system, you MUST get input from the members on what that will look like.

I encourage associations that want to update or modernize their chapter systems to take a step back and examine them with fresh eyes and "beginner's mind." Evaluate everything as if it is the first time you are seeing it and are just beginning to understand it. Modernizing does not necessarily mean completely remaking or throwing out your network. It might be that you need to streamline your system or revise your governance.

This fresh examination may reveal you **do need** to completely remake your system. If that is the case, you need to cultivate patience because it is not a short-term project.

Some questions to consider:

- What do you have in place that is working?
- Can resources be redirected to be more effective?
- What isn't working? Why isn't it working? How can you fix it or remove it?
- Can you improve relationships with unhappy volunteer leaders and chapter staff?
- How does the chapter network tie into your governance system? Can you revise one without updating the other?
- Is it really bad, or are you going through a rough patch with your chapter relationships?
- Are you asking too much of your chapter leaders?

Modernizing the system is important, but make sure you fully understand your motivation for modernizing. It could be as simple as resource allocation, or as complicated as repairing relationships.

Either way, give yourself credit for what you are doing well.

Cecilia Sepp, CAE, ACNP

Chapter Structures Continue to Frustrate Associations – So Let them Go

I am a Chapter Relations Professional at heart, having served as one earlier in my career for over 15 years at several organizations. Working with the local groups and members was a rewarding and sometimes challenging experience. I learned a lot and I believe it helped the organizations where I worked thrive.

However, all good things must come to an end, and it is time to purposefully abandon the way we currently do things with chapters. It is time for chapters as we know them to end.

Letting go of the current tenet that chapters must be a miniature version of the national association will allow us to create a new system that is adaptive to the fast moving 21st Century.

The reason you are finding your systems cumbersome, burdensome, and unattractive to today's volunteer leaders is because these are based on designs from the 19th century.

When put into historical context, **membership associations are using systems designed in an era when travel took long periods of time, there were few if any telephones, telegrams were expensive, and most business was conducted via correspondence** that took days or weeks to get somewhere. I call this the era of the mini-me association; smaller versions of the organization were formed across the country (and sometimes across the world) because of the lengthy periods it took to communicate.

Therefore, you had local boards of directors, local committees, local bank accounts, and activities that happened in isolation without a lot of support from the national or international association. Large conferences or conventions were held every three to five years, and sometimes lasted for months.

As time passed, and travel became easier and communication became faster, the same system was left in place. *The adaptation to current ways of doing things didn't happen. And it still hasn't.*

What today's associations should consider is throwing out this old system completely and **removing the burden of being a part-time unpaid employee from volunteer leaders at the state and local level**. To do that, think differently. What would actually work for your group? Do you need to waste all this time and money on a system that doesn't fit in the 21st Century?

Chapters do not have to be difficult. **Frankly, chapters aren't really necessary any longer.** What you need is a structure that supports local networking with little or no responsibility on the local members/volunteers.

Some people will see nothing but obstacles in changing the system. But what if you let your imagination connect with what people really need instead of "that's the way we've always done it"? Stop controlling and start building. Sometimes the best way to win is to surrender.

Cecilia Sepp, CAE, ACNP
Re-Imagining Chapter Systems

Chapter networks can and should change over time. The solutions will be as unique as your association and will depend on the support and interest of members.

Things to consider when working toward updating, modernizing, or revolutionizing your chapter network:

1. Culture: what emotional attachments to your current way of doing things exist among members and volunteer leaders?
2. The "Why" of your Chapters: why do you have chapters?
3. The "What" of your Chapters: what do you ask of them? What do you do for them?
4. The "Who" of your Chapters: are they the same people participating over years or do the chapters attract new members and inspire new leaders for the association?
5. The "How" of your Chapters: are your chapters delivering value or are they doing a lot of administrative tasks?
6. Is anyone having any fun?

The current chapter network: What is the profile of each chapter? How does each chapter operate? What is similar and different within the chapters? Are there programs/services offered locally that could be modeled across the network? How does performance compare with self-managed (volunteer run) chapters to paid staff and the AMC-supported chapters?

Work through these major areas to assess what you have now and where you could go:

Unique Chapters: What is the experience of members in different geographic areas? If you have chapters based on a type of employment, such as Government Employees, how does their experience and support compare?

Chapter Resources: How do chapters use their resources (e.g., money)? What funding is available from national in support of chapters? What services do chapters receive for a fee? What services do chapters receive for *no* fee? How does the national association staff work with and support chapters? What is the level of awareness of the services available to your chapters? Do chapters seek additional resources that are not currently provided (e.g., training materials such as webinars and toolkits)?

Chapter Perceptions of the National/Chapter Relationship: What do chapter leaders of all types see within the national/chapter relationship? Is it positive? Is it negative? Is it collaborative? Do chapters feel they are "told" what to do versus a partnership relationship? Do chapters want more or less support?

Governance Structure Impact: Does the association fulfill its promise of representing chapters? Should the processes change? If the chapter model changed, what might be the impact on the association and its work? What will an affiliation agreement include in the future? What requirements are needed? What responsibilities will be assigned to the chapter and to the national association?

Chapters and the Member Experience: What value do members perceive from chapters? Is this where they participate the most? Or do they look to the national association to provide value? Would fewer chapters serve the membership better?

Cecilia Sepp, CAE, ACNP
A New Way Forward

For years I have advocated that we need to change the way we do things with our local chapters. The model needs to be revamped, expectations need to be adjusted, and our attitude needs to change. If we move from control to collaboration, both the national association and the chapters will benefit.

Keep in mind this thought: "To conquer others is to have power. To conquer yourself is to have strength." Lao Tzu, Tao Te Ching (The Way of Virtue)

Attitude is everything so don't be tyrranical in your chapter system. Focusing on punishment and retribution for missed deadlines rather than focusing on positive outcomes turns people off. I can attest that a missed report deadline has yet to bring down a chapter or the association it is part of – at least not yet.

If we overcome our negative mindset about chapters and see them as valuable partners, we will make the work of the chapter relations professional easier and increase the value of the member experience. Stop complaining and start explaining to your chapters why you ask them to do what they do. Understanding leads to teamwork.

Rather than making chapter leaders deal with lists of tasks that do nothing to move their chapter forward like filing multiple reports, let's make it as easy as possible for chapter leaders to produce meaningful programming, organize networking events, and share knowledge. Our volunteers signed up to share their time and energy, not get treated like an unpaid full-time employee. Support, don't scold.

It's your association's system, so you can create the one that works for you and your local members. You don't need to follow the traditional mini-me model. You can create local networking groups that don't have boards, committees, or bank accounts. This could be designed as a local volunteer experience that does not require "officialdom" but does create a way for you to identify future leaders.

Working with local members to make things happen outside a formal structure is doable and will remove a lot of the stress of the traditional chapter system. It will be a lot more fun for everyone too!

But to do things differently we need to remove the current model. This requires commitment to a longer-term project, as it will likely take 18 months to 3 years to complete from concept to implementation. The timeline will be affected by how many chapters you have, the current structure for each chapter, how long it takes to get buy-in from local leaders, the activities put in place to review and assess the current system, and the review process for the recommendations.

When changing anything where people have titles, leadership roles, and influence, you will need to delicately manage the emotions of loss, fear, and anger. People will feel they are losing something rather than gaining something.

This is why you need to include as many local leaders as possible to gather input, suggestions, and needs. Relationship management is crucial in revamping any system but it's especially important with a chapter network. Your volunteers have put in a lot of time and energy making their chapter what it is; make sure they know the only thing they are losing is responsibility. What they are gaining are opportunities to do more, be more, and see more.

If we want our chapter relationships to go from frustrating to fruitful, we need to remove the obstacles to achievement. We need to build the positive collaboration that will lead us to valuable local activities. **The current chapter model gets in the way of positive outcomes.**

Let's sunset this system that no longer serves us and put in the time and effort to create the system that works for today, not the 19th century. Fruitful relationships live in the present, not the past.

About the Author

Cecilia Sepp, CAE, ACNP
Principal & Founder
Rogue Tulips Consulting

Cecilia is a recognized authority in nonprofit organization management and a leader who translates vision into action. She shares her expertise as a consultant, writer, speaker, podcast host, and skilled facilitator adept in all aspects of nonprofit management.

Her company, Rogue Tulips Consulting, provides myriad services for nonprofit organizations including executive leadership services, mentorship programs and education, content development/communications, and staff compensation studies.

Cecilia regularly posts on her blog, "Going Rogue," which addresses the spectrum of nonprofit management issues as well as societal quandaries. She is the author of a book on Chapter Relations titled, "Association Chapter Systems: From Frustrating to Fruitful," published by Broken Column Press.

She is the producer and host of "Radio Free 501c," a weekly podcast bringing together nonprofit and for-profit business professionals from around the United States and the world to discuss issues of importance to nonprofit organizations.

Her passion for the profession of nonprofit management led her to create an education program, Rogue Tulips Education, to support nonprofit management executives in their professional development. The flagship course is "The Ethical Nonprofit: Ethics for 501c Professionals," an ethics program for nonprofit executives and their organizations. Rogue Tulips Education offers study groups, courses, topic-specific webinars, and individual coaching.

Cecilia earned the Certified Association Executive (CAE) designation in 2015, and the Advanced Certified Nonprofit Professional (ACNP) designation in 2023. She also earned certificates in nonprofit accounting, diversity equity & inclusion, and virtual event management. She was recognized by Association Women Technology Champions (AWTC) as a 2022 AWTC Champion.

More about Cecilia: https://www.linkedin.com/in/ceciliasepp/

Info about Rogue Tulips Consulting: https://www.roguetulips.com/

Read the blog "Going Rogue": https://roguetulips.com/blog

Learn about the Education Program: https://roguetulips.com/education

The Podcast: Radio Free 501c: https://www.roguetulips.com/podcast

Made in the USA
Columbia, SC
22 November 2024

47362669R00059